(Non-Fungible Tokens)
2021-2022

A Beginner's Guide to the Future of Trading Art,
Collectibles
and Digital Assets

STELLAR MOON PUBLISHING

Disclaimer

Introduction

This hype is unparalleled: The demand for NFT is high and rising, the market for trading digital assets have become a lucrative business.

Artists, investors and collectors are sensing new opportunities, because the virtual tokens are opening the gates to a potentially huge future market. An NFT by graphic artist Mike "Beeple" Winkelmann has already fetched 69 million US dollars, and memes are also changing hands for six-figure prices.

What exactly are NFTs and what can they be used for? The term "Non-Fungible Token" (NFT) is an abbreviation for "Non-Fungible Token."

Unlike Bitcoin or any other banknote, NFTs are distinct, meaning that they are completely different and not interchangeable.
Because of this, one NFT may be nearly worthless, whereas another may be auctioned off to a Singaporean entrepreneur for $69 million.

So, while cryptocurrencies can be traded in the same way as regular money, NFT demonstrate legal ownership as well as ownership of digital works and media. NFTs can also be cryptographically signed, granting them ownership.

Whether it's images, music, virtual event tickets, or usernames and items in computer games: All of these digital goods are tradable thanks to NFTs, which also certify legally valid ownership claims.

The ownership of NFTS are currently primarily stored as a component of the Ethereum blockchain.

This book about NFTs has been compiled by Stellar Moon Publishing's crypto experts and will teach you everything you need to know about the future of trading digital goods.

We've got you covered, from current trends to everything you need to know about buying or selling NFTs!

Table of Contents

Our books

Check out our other book to learn more about crypto trading, investing, how to make profit and essential tips and strategies for a fail-proof start in the crypto universe.

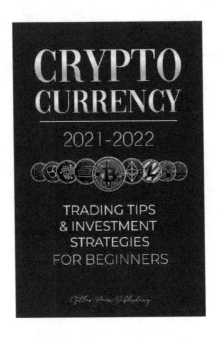

Join the exclusive Stellar Moon Publishing Circle!

You'll get instant access to the mailing list with updates from our experts every week!

Sign up here today:

https://campsite.bio/stellarmoonpublishing

What are NFTs exactly?

As we said in the introduction already, a NFT stands for "Non-Fungible Token" and wit that term, it describes a non-exchangeable value.

Thus, an NFT stands in contrast to exchangeable values, such as a currency. Fungibility, or interchangeability, is a term used in economics and finance. It is the ability to exchange an item with a similar item of comparable value. For example, four 5-euro bills can be exchanged for one 20-euro bill without any change in value. Non-"fungible" values, NFTs, are the exact opposite. Each NFT is unique and cannot be replaced by another item.

A good example of such items that can't be replaced are, for example, famous paintings. You can't just replace an original van Gogh painting with a poster from the museum store. The poster does not have the same value as the real painting.

The difference between fungible and non-fungible

To understand what makes NFT so unique, one must first understand the distinction between fungible and non-fungible materials. When something is fungible, it means that it is interchangeable in a homogeneous manner. Currency notes or precious metals are examples of this in the real world: one gram of pure gold is worth the same as another gram of pure gold. And it doesn't matter if you give someone a ten-euro note if they don't return the exact same note.

9

When something is not fungible, all of this changes. Although two objects may appear identical at first glance, they both possess unique information or properties that render them irreplaceable or non-interchangeable.

A plane ticket is an example of a non-fungible good. At first glance, flight tickets appear to be the same, but each ticket contains a different passenger name, destination, and seat number.

As a result, exchanging one flight ticket for another could have serious ramifications. In the digital realm, it is analogous to NFTs. Internet domains are another example, because each domain can only exist once.

What is the difference between non-fungible and fungible tokens?

Non-fungible tokens can limit and represent things in digital space in a unique way. Many other cryptocurrencies and tokens, such as Bitcoin and Ether, are fungible. You wouldn't notice a difference if you sent someone ether and received ether in return.

The same is true for tokens: the majority of tokens are currently based on Ethereum's ERC-20 standard. For the sake of simplicity, consider each of these tokens to be a ten-euro note. If you send this token to someone and then receive another one a week later, this token is identical to the other.

With non-fungible tokens, all of that changes. Currently, the majority of NFTs on the Ethereum Blockchain adhere to the ERC-721 standard. This standard's tokens can be compared to Pokémon or Yu-Gi-Oh trading cards. Each token has its own set of characteristics and a different level of rarity.

There is another significant difference that you should be aware of. Fungible tokens are divisible, which means that a fraction of a Bitcoin or another ERC-20 token can be sent or owned. Similar to cash, you can pay with a ten-euro note and get change back.

Non-fungible tokens, on the other hand, cannot be shared and must be purchased or sold in full. Similarly to trading cards, where nobody would buy just half a card.

Use cases for NFTs

The applications for NFT are virtually limitless. Non-fungible tokens, in fact, can serve as the foundation for a new digital economy based on blockchain technology. The real world and the digital world can coexist with the help of NFT.

Aside from mapping scarcity and uniqueness in exclusively digital space, the digitization process of objects and assets from the physical world into the virtual one is also greatly facilitated.

Games

The sale of rare weapons or skins in popular games such as World of Warcraft, Fortnite, CS: GO, and League of Legends is currently prohibited. It is also not possible to combine items or skins from different games. It would be possible to transfer items and clearly assign ownership rights using NFTs. This would alleviate some of the most significant annoyances experienced by avid gamers.

Art

Protecting their copyrights and making money in the digital age is frequently a nightmare for artists.

Someone can use NFTs to purchase a work of art and present it in a virtual space, with the blockchain proving ownership.

This allows artists to protect their copyrights and keep a larger portion of the sale proceeds. Furthermore, an NFT can be configured in such a way that it generates a recurring source of income from each subsequent sale of the NFT. Several NFTs have recently been sold for hundreds of thousands of euros, and many expect the art NFT sector to grow dramatically in the future.

Collectibles

NFTs are already being used to create completely new types of collectibles, as seen with the CryptoKitties, the Fantasy Football Game Sorare, and the NBA Top Shot by Dapper Labs.

Sorare, for example, allows users to purchase tokenized versions of their favorite players. The concept is similar to the Panini collection pictures that many people recall from their childhood. The same principle is now being applied in the digital world in the form of digital collectibles, which digitally represent possession of a trading card.

Financial assets

There is a sizable NFT market for virtual assets. It is possible to purchase land from virtual land on platforms such as Decentraland and Cryptovoxels.

These lots, like real-world lots, have distinct characteristics.

These properties are already being traded for tens of thousands of euros in virtual worlds. Furthermore, the Unstoppable Domains website has tokenized domain names. Any name on a website can be converted into an NFT that anyone can freely trade.

Although this area of NFTs is still in its infancy, real assets such as works of art or record contracts can be tokenized as NFTs. The NFTs are used to prove (partially) ownership of a work of art or to regulate royalties claims.

Identities

Everyone is unique, from their appearance to their educational qualifications and medical history. It is possible to tokenize this identity using non-fungible tokens. This means that all data available about a person can be represented as an NFT, allowing people to regain control of their data.

Why should you buy NFTs?

An image can be viewed, copied, and saved online by almost anyone. An NFT, on the other hand, provides the purchaser with something that cannot be duplicated. Specifically, ownership of a work. NFTs can be compared to collectibles.

Like paintings, stamps, and comic books, but in digital form. However, at first glance, it appears that you are purchasing something that is already freely available on the Internet. For example, photographs and videos. A LeBron James slam dunk was recently sold as a trading card for $208,000. The video, however, is freely available on the Internet.

The issue here is that a collectible in real life is tangible. A painting, such as the Mona Lisa, may appear differently than a poster copy. In contrast, digital NFTs are visually indistinguishable from their copies. Only the use of underlying encryption ensures that it is the original.

So, an NFT is only valuable because others place a fictitious value on it.

In the context of the LeBron dunk, this means that the trading card that includes the video is the official NBA clip.

Having the official clip adds prestige to the card, increasing its value. Only those who have this card have true ownership of the clip. Everything else is a knockoff.

How is it ensured that originals are not simply copied?

The Ethereum blockchain includes NFTs. This is the fundamental framework for the cryptocurrency "Ether," which is the world's second most valuable after Bitcoin. While other blockchains have now implemented NFTs, the Ethereum network remains the largest NFT platform.

As a result, NFTs are a type of cryptocurrency. They are, however, distinct from Bitcoin, Ether, and other cryptocurrencies. They have a digital signature, similar to a great painter's signature. This means that the original can always be identified as such, even if there are many similar copies of it.

The blockchain is analogous to an accounting system for accounts, but it is entirely online and digital. It is a safe method of tracking the sale of digital items. NFTs, on the other hand, are stored as a string of numbers and letters, as opposed to an account book.

This virtual certificate stores information about the owner or holder of an NFT, as well as the date of sale and to whom it was sold.

The transaction of money spent on an NFT is added to the list of previous transactions with the purchase. Storing this data in the blockchain ensures the NFT's authenticity and uniqueness.

Who needs NFTs in the first place?

This solves a problem that many creative people face on the Internet.

It enables them to ensure that their works are not simply copied and distributed on the Internet. The value of a one-of-a-kind original rises as a result of its creation. Only one authentic original of each NFT can ever exist.

As a result, the goal is to create artificial scarcity. A good example is a streaming service such as Spotify. Musicians only receive a small amount of money for their songs on Spotify. However, if a song is only available as an NFT as an original on the Internet once, its value skyrockets.

There may be multiple copies of the song, but only one person may own the original. Furthermore, the creator of an NFT can stipulate in it, for example, that a certain amount is paid to him or her every time the token is resold.

Creators can now offer items for which there was previously no sales platform thanks to NFTs. GIFs or stickers, for example, to send via Messenger.

In theory, NFTs can be anything that can be digitally stored. However, at the moment, the emphasis is on digital art.

NFTs are driven by speculation.

NFTs are also a way for unskilled samplers to make money. On the art market, one can buy an NFT and speculate that its value will rise.

Someone, for example, bought a "Gucci Ghost" for 3600 US dollars on the "Nifty Gateway" website and now wants 16.300 US dollars for it. The original fee for creating the image was $200 US dollars.

What types of NFTs are there?

NFTs are used, digital art and sports collectibles, but also video games. One of the first applications that made use of the NFT principle was the digital collecting game "CryptoKitties" from 2017. Game players could buy, trade and breed collectible cats. Each new cat was an NFT, thus ensuring authenticity and uniqueness.

The original copy of "Nyan Cat," a popular 2011 meme that was part cat, part pop-tart (an American sweet pastry), was sold in an online auction in February for 300 ether (approximately $600,000).

Kings of Leon, a band from the United States, raised $2 million by releasing a digital-only album.

In March, Twitter founder Jack Dosey's first tweet sold for $2.5 million. Even the New York Times sells articles as NFT for a pittance of $560,000.

Also in March, the auction house Christie's auctioned off its first purely digital work of art in the form of an NFT for 69 million U.S. dollars - a picture collage called "The First 5000 Days," which had been in the works for 13 years.

The US NBA, for example, shows how NFTs function as trading cards with Top Shot. Users can use it to collect short videos of basketball highlights. Since October 2020, NBA Top Shot has generated more than 333 million US dollars.

Of course, the fact that an NFT is unique does not mean that each object exists only once. Collectible cards, for example, can exist multiple times, just like in real life. Thanks to the blockchain, however, it is possible to track when each individual card has changed hands.

Why are some NFTs worth millions of euros?

This is where things get exciting and potentially dangerous. Opinions on NFT vary greatly, just as they do on Bitcoin and other cryptocurrencies. Some see the tokens as an unavoidable revolution in the art world, while others see them as a gimmick with enormous loss potential.

Although you can't hang NFT on your wall, the tokens have already sold for exorbitant prices: Jack Dorsey's first tweet sold for $2.5 million, a collection by Rick and Morty creator Justin Roiland sold for $2.3 million, and "Disaster Girl" Zo Roth sold an NFT of her memes for as much as $500,000.

Such large sums are only possible when a corresponding demand exists, which is currently particularly high due to the hype surrounding NFT. Speculators and collectors are drawn to this.

Furthermore, digital art is unquestionably a powerful market of the future, so NFT is bound to jolt some people in the art industry awake.

Of course, this is not a guarantee of instant wealth; bubbles can form in NFT, and large losses can occur - but so can massive profits.

Is there a future for NFTs?

We can only speculate, but everything appears to be pointing in that direction at the moment. If digital art is viable in the future, then NFTs are likely to be as well.

Many other areas of application are theoretically possible. The tokens could be used as forgery-proof tickets for events ranging from concerts to water parks, in addition to serving as a certificate of authenticity.

Non-digital objects could be verified with them one day, and they could also be used to identify people, for example, with authorities or public offices.

There are also computer games in which NFT take the form of items, characters, or virtual land. Binance, the world's largest cryptocurrency trading platform, has also entered the fray: Noch in June 2021, a separate market for crypto-arts will be established.

In this regard, one must consider both the sale of high-priced premium items and the sale of Otto-Normal-Products: A second market place for everyone should allow for the exchange of shaky goods.

Binance will start with a 1% commission, implying that the company is betting on a growing market.

So it seems that NFTs are here to stay, and might be a very interesting and profitable investment option.

NFT Issues

Who guarantees that a work remains unique?

Buying an NFT from an artist, by the way, does not mean that they lose their copyright in it. That's one of the potential problems with NFTs. After all, what if someone decides to simply sell the same artwork you've already bought a second time?

So far, the young NFT market does not offer a solution to this. Therefore, it is important to make sure that the person selling is trustworthy. The first port of call should therefore be well-known sales platforms such as Nifty Gateway, OpenSea and Rarible.

Extremely high energy consumption

NFTs, like other cryptocurrencies, require increasing amounts of energy because blockchains are extremely hungry for computing power. As a result, some creators have already stated that they will no longer create NFTs in the future in order to avoid further increasing energy demand.

However, in any case this would have a problem we would have to face at some point. It can not be evaded, it is simply a challenge in our evolution that we will have to overcome.

We have to switch to renewable energy sources as soon as possible and in essence, cryptocurrency could help with that problem, because of the urgency and the fact that at some point, fossil fuels will run out.

NFTs are not protected from deletion

Instead of, say, purchasing a painting to hang in your living room, when you purchase an NFT, you are only purchasing a type of title deed, not the NFT itself.

The blockchain deed contains all of the information about an NFT's authorship, transactions, and ownership, and as such, it cannot be deleted. The NFT, on the other hand, must be stored on a server somewhere.

Purchasing an NFT essentially grants you access to the NFT. If the website is deleted or the server where the NFT is stored is relocated, this code will take you nowhere. In this case, owning an NFT is essentially equivalent to owning a dead link on the Internet.

The issue of value

It is also questionable whether the possession of a unique NFT alone makes it valuable. It is true that a buyer or purchaser holds the original, genuine NFT. However, because it is digital art, that person cannot stop others from copying the image and sharing it online.

So are NFTs an evolving digital bubble? Investors continue to believe NFTs are the next digital revolution. But there are still many unanswered questions. If you buy an NFT, who guarantees it will be worth the money? The value of an object is only as long as there are people spending money on it. Like other cryptocurrency, NFTs have no equivalent value in the real world. If, for example, everyone decided from one day to the next to turn all their NFTs into money, who would buy them?

Gas fees

Because of the insanely high selling prices that make headlines, many people are venturing into trading digital collector tokens. But things don't always go as planned.

Robert Martin, a senior content strategist at Kapwing, a digital marketing platform, experimented with trading NFTs. He tells Insider that the process of buying and selling is not as simple as it appears.

"It has a Wild West feel to it," Martin says after paying a more than $200 transaction fee known as a gas fee.

Ether (ETH), WAX, and FLOW are the most commonly used crypto currencies on NFT trading platforms. Users who choose Ethereum, the first digital currency, incur certain costs. The so-called gas fees are a transaction fee that covers the energy costs associated with processing and validating blockchain transactions. Gas prices vary depending on the time of day.

Martin, for example, paid about $30 for an NFT on the trading platform Rarible using the cryptocurrency Ethereum. Even after a buyer bid more than three times the original price within 24 hours, he ended up losing more than $200 on his digital gathering token.

Although transaction fees vary by trading platform, many popular websites charge users a gas fee for processing and validating a transaction on the blockchain, as well as a price for selling and buying an NFT.

In addition, most platforms require a digital wallet, so users should factor in exchange fees for digital coins like ether.

Martin was taken aback when his digital wallet, Rainbow Wallet, charged him nearly $80 to exchange Wrapped ether (WETH) for regular ether (ETH).

"I had to pay to receive WETH, but it was unclear whether I or the sender should pay the fee," Martin explains.

Martin, as a new user, didn't immediately understand what the gas fees were. As a result, the transaction appeared to him to be a good deal; he would sell an NFT in less than a day for nearly three times the original price. However, the additional expenses ended up being greater than the original purchase price.

While Martin's digital wallet had a description of the fees in the fine print, it would have been helpful if there had been a warning or notification about the fees before he made the purchase.

"Gas fees can be a risk for new users," said Martin. "A lot more information and guidance is needed on this." Everything appears to be set up for people who are already familiar with the crypto world."

Rodriguez-Fraile said he knew Beeple's work would one day be extremely valuable, but he had no idea it would rise from $67 to $6.6 million in a matter of months.

"I didn't want to be someone who buys something expecting to make a quick profit, but I also don't like losing money," Rodriguez-Fraile says. "I received a higher bid on another Beeple piece, but I kept it because of its historical significance." The only reason I sold the artwork 'Crossroads' was because I thought it could give an important push to the development of digital art."

Cryptokitties & Ethereum

CryptoKitties, a game built on Ethereum that allows players to collect, breed, and exchange virtual cats, was one of the first NFT projects to garner a lot of attention.

Each CryptoKitty can have a mix of characteristics such as age, breed, and color. As a result, each is unique and cannot be exchanged for another. They are also indivisible, which means that a CryptoKitty token cannot be divided into divisible parts (like the gwei for ether).

CryptoKitties gained notoriety after it overloaded the Ethereum blockchain due to the amount of activity it generated in the network. The All-Time High (ATH) for the number of daily transactions on the Ethereum blockchain is still around the peak of CryptoKitties' popularity as of February 2020. It is obvious that the game has had a significant impact on the Ethereum network, but other factors, such as the rise of Initial Coin Offerings, have also played a role (ICO).

You can read more about the future developments of crypto kitties in the chapter about the FLOW blockchain. The Flow blockchain has been created by the cryptokitties developers, due to the shortcomings of the Ethereum blockchain

Where you can buy NFTs?

These are our top 5 market places where you can buy and sell your NFT digital goods. From videos, GIF images, trading cards and memes. All sorts of digital art can find a new owner on these market places.

5. Enjin Marketplace: A gaming marketplace

The official marketplace for Enjin-based NFTs is the Enjin Marketplace. Users can easily and quickly trade Non Fungible Tokens via the website. Enjin also published one of the first trading venues for NFTs and is widely regarded as the creator of the ERC-1155 standard. ENJ tokens are required to purchase NFTs. You'll also need Ethereum to process transactions.

The Enjin platform is designed specifically for gamers, with various items that can be used in multiple games.

The Enjin Marketplace has a large trading volume, lists thousands of items, and has an easy-to-use web interface.

According to DappReview, there are over 1 billion ERC-1155 items for which over $1 million has already been deposited with ENJ.

4. Rarible: Earn RARI tokens by trading NFTs.

NFTs can be created and traded using Rarible. RARI, the platform's governance token, is also available.

This token enables you to vote on important issues. Users have the option of keeping the generated NFTs, giving them away, or selling and buying them on the marketplace. In addition, Rarible platform users will receive RARI tokens as a reward for trading NFTs.

3. SuperRare: The marketplace for artists

SuperRare, as the name implies, deals with extremely rare art. As a result, it is an NFT marketplace that specializes in digital artwork.

With social profiles, a mobile app, live auctions, and advanced payment options, the platform distinguishes itself from other NFT marketplaces.

2. Decentraland: A virtual marketplace

Decentraland is best described as a Minecraft-like virtual world where NFTs can be traded. Users can also acquire one-of-a-kind plots that they can freely develop. In the virtual world, you can also play a variety of games.

There is currently a Halloween special where you can win boxes containing various items:

MANA token holders can use the token to pay for various NFTs in Decentraland. Furthermore, MANA grants users governance rights in Decentraland. This allows the community to vote on permitted NFT contracts, marketplace rules, and other Decentraland processes.

1. Opensea: A global marketplace for non-financial transactions

To date, Opensea is the largest trading center for NFTs, allowing trading in all types of NFTs. As a result, Opensea users can trade, buy, and sell art, game items, collectibles, domain names, and so on.

All other marketplaces pale in comparison to the breadth of the offer. Furthermore, the platform includes a number of auction functions and is fully integrated into the crypto infrastructure.

Despite being the largest NFT marketplace in the crypto space, Opensea does not have its own token and is currently only used as a trading interface for NFTs. NFTs from Decentraland, SuperRare, and Enjin, for example, can be traded on Opensea.

OpenSea

OpenSea is a decentralized marketplace for non-fungible tokens (NFT) for buying, selling and trading these unique tokens. They themselves claim to be the largest platform for trading NFTs. For the first time, you can own a digital product.

In the past, we see that existing works of art, such as images, can be easily copied, which means that no more credits go to the effective artist. With blockchain technology, all information about these NFTs is recorded so that the rightful owner can always be found in the source code.

These digital items were previously part of a company's data. Let's look at popular games like Fortnite. You can go and change the outfit of your favorite avatar, but it will never be yours. This is because there are rules imposed from the central board that determine what is possible in the platform and what is not.

Unlike NFTs, you can go and design an outfit that does not belong to the platform, but that you own. A platform like OpenSea immediately shows the freedom everyone has regarding designing and trading NFTs. OpenSea has more than 14 million items listed and more are added every day.

Before you can trade NFTs on OpenSea, you need an Ethereum wallet. This is a wallet linked to ERC20 tokens on Ethereum's blockchain. You can learn more on buying NFTs with a wallet in the next chapter.

How to use OpenSea

There are many NFTs in circulation at OpenSea so it is important that you can navigate easily. Via the Browse tab you can search for items. If you know the name of the particular artwork, you can navigate directly. If not, you can use the filter options.

For example, you can choose between art but also collectibles or sports, among others. If you choose a market segment here, you will immediately see the top collection and trending items. These appear at the top of your search results.

By activating additional filters, you can choose to immediately show the NFTs with the highest price, or items that are about to expire. Are you only willing to buy an item that is on sale? There are several filtering options so everyone can easily navigate the network.

The network also uses different statuses per item. At the top, you can filter between types of NFT by default, but on the left side of the menu you can choose different statuses:

Buy now

These are the works that are immediately offered for sale. These are works that have been available for some time and obviously this is the largest group of NFTs.

New

Are you looking for the latest NFTs on the platform?

Through the filter 'New' you can see which works have recently been added to the platform.

Through this filter you can see if there are new trends in the world of NFT. This is not only useful to buy them, but also to get started as a creator.

On Auction

It also happens more often that artists do not opt for a typical sale, but decide to auction their work through an auction. This has a fixed end date. When this has passed, the work is sold to the highest bidder. For each item you can see what the highest bid was and who made that bid.

Has Offers

Not every work is interesting and gets bids, that would be too good. You can therefore choose to only show digital assets that already have offers. This way you don't endlessly scroll through new works that are not interesting but keep coming back.

These filters are not separate but can be combined with each other. For example, you can filter on new items that have already had offers.

Why is this interesting? So you can see what the demand is, how many people are interested in a particular NFT or art form.

You can then get to work creating an NFT yourself and offer it for sale on the platform. For example, we saw in April 2021 that there is an increasing interest in the new Polkamon.

How can you buy or sell NFTS?

In order to buy, sell or create an NFT you need cryptocurrency, a wallet and some other steps to get started. We explained this process in 4 easy steps below, and this should get you well on your way to your first digital art ownership.

Step 1: Make a wallet

To create and sell NFTs, you must first obtain a cryptocurrency. Which, in turn, can only be kept in a digital money purse (wallet). That means you must first obtain the wallet. There are various providers for various currencies. However, because major trading platforms are typically built on the Ethereum blockchain, you will also require the corresponding currency: ETH. On the ethereum.org page, you can find out which wallets are suitable for this. There's a useful wallet finder there.

You can also look at the major trading platforms to see which wallets are compatible with the service. The wallets, by the way, are only used to interact with your crypto account. As a result, switching providers is simple.

Please keep in mind that each blockchain has its own set of NFT standards. That is, if you create an NFT artwork on the Ethereum blockchain, you can only sell it on platforms that support Ethereum. Binance Smart Chain, Polkadot, Tron, and Tezos are some Ethereum alternatives. It is not difficult to provide an NFT on multiple blockchains.

Step 2: Purchase cryptocurrency

You must now purchase the appropriate currency after deciding on a currency and wallet. This is usually done directly through the wallet application. Various payment methods are available, depending on the provider. This step is required because trading platforms charge fees for the creation of NFTs. A budget of around € 100 should be sufficient to get you started.

Step 3: Connect the wallet to a NFT marketplace

The following step is to select a trading venue for your NFT plant. There is now a diverse range of providers in this area. Rarible and OpenSea are two of the most popular. Both platforms have the Create or Connect Wallet function. There, you must select your corresponding wallet, after which you can connect by scanning a QR code.

Step 4: Set up and sell or buy NFTs

Now we get to the really fun part of the tutorial: making NFTs. In theory, the procedure is very straightforward. You must first upload your work (picture, song, or video) to the appropriate trading venue in a suitable file format if you have anything that you would like to sell. Rarible, for example, accepts the following file formats: PNG, GIF, WEBP, MP4, or MP3.

You can then specify the sale's specifics. So it doesn't matter if it's an auction or a fixed-price sale. You can also establish royalties.

This means that every time the artwork is sold, you will receive a percentage of the sale price. When you're finished with the specifications, click " Create " to upload your artwork.

You are now able to sell your NFT. However, it is not necessary to sell the NFTs. You can also make them without any intention of selling them and upload them to your online gallery.

NFTs, by the way, are not bound to the platform on which they are created. The NFT is stored on the respective blockchain and can be accessed via a variety of platforms.

As we already explained a bit how to use the platform Opensea, here we want to explain shortly how you can buy NFTs on this platform or create a listing to sell your own.

Buying NFTs on OpenSea

Buying is of course also an important aspect with a trading platform like OpenSea.

The question is of course not only why you buy an NFT, but also how. First of all you obviously need to make sure your wallet is connected and that you have enough capital to buy an NFT, including the gas and transaction costs.

At the overview page you get detailed information about the sale but also about the artist. This way you can see which artworks the artist has made yet. Are you a collector? This way you can quickly buy multiple items from the same artist. In the current example, it is a new item that has just been listed on the platform and has currently been viewed 13 times.

We see that the artist wants to sell this item for $50. Are you willing to buy this for the full amount? If not, you can also choose to make an informal bid.

At the bottom you can see a trading history where you can see whether other interested parties have made a bid and by how much.

This will also give you an idea whether the artist has set a realistic price.

Create your own NFT listing

OpenSea not only wants to be a marketplace for NFTs, they also share knowledge on how to get started creating your own items.

In the menu at create, you can suddenly navigate to 'develop with us'. Here Open Sea offers you numerous tutorials to get started in an easy way. Of course you can also choose to create your own NFT separately from these manuals.

The advantage is that there are no rules about these items. Do you choose to make an animated version of a static image? Would you rather create an abstract work of art and offer it on the platform? Everyone is free to create what he or she wants.

You can then also create your NFT outside of the platform and then trade it on OpenSea.

When you are logged into your wallet, for example MetaMask, you can choose in your own personal dashboard to create a new NFT or to start uploading an already created NFT.

Describe your artwork or your item and go ahead and create it yourself. Did you create your NFT through another platform or did you create it yourself using, for example, graphic programs? The nice thing is that really anything can be an NFT. Do you want to make a childishly simple work in Paint? It may be that you can sell it for a nice amount of money, provided there is interest.

You can upload your NFT here from your computer and it will appear immediately in your own personal dashboard. Your digital artwork is on your computer and by uploading it to OpenSea, you turn it into an NFT.

Again emphasizing here that there are no regulations for designing an NFT, that is just the freedom that prevails in the decentralized network where everyone can decide what they want to create and what they want to offer and trade on the platform.

While some NFTs focus mainly on use cases, think of unique avatars that can be used on a gaming platform, an NFT can just as easily be a static image that needs imagination to interpret what it represents.

Are you creatively inclined and want to get started designing and trading NFTs yourself? Then OpenSea is a user-friendly and effective platform. You can view not only what items are being traded, but more importantly the developments taking place in the world of NFT.

Discover the latest items and list your own unique token. So with all this knowledge it shouldn't be too hard to start your first trade!

The use cases of NFTs are only increasing and evolving to the point where there are almost no limitations. There are more and more possibilities to integrate these use cases in another platform.

So far it is mainly the in-game industry that is gaining popularity but also art, collectibles or the latest trend: Polkamons.

There will certainly be more things and variants to come, especially as the industry continues to evolve with decentralized funding (DeFi). More integration also means more NFT asset classes and an expansion of the possibilities and number of integration platforms.

There are several protocols vying for NFTs but a centralized place like OpenSea for offering and trading NFTs will only gain popularity as the use cases increase. One advantage is the high degree of freedom where anyone can be an artist to create an NFT.

Enjin coin

We've already given a short explanation about on the Enjin coin and the Enjin marketplace, as a platform for games in our top 5 marketplaces for NFTs.

So, to summarize it, before we delve deeper into Enjin; Enjin Coin is a blockchain gaming platform focused on creating digital collectibles that are truly owned by the user. The crypto project has been on many people's radar since 2019 as they have partnered with Samsung. Enjin does this through ERC-1155 tokens, an enhanced version of ERC20 and ERC721 tokens.

Enjin Coin is a cryptocurrency for the gaming industry. The team wants this to be the currency that will be used everywhere within the gaming industry.

Besides this crypto currency, they also offer an all-in-one platform for developing your own game, based on blockchain technology. This platform is free and anyone can use it.

Currently, they already have more than 250,000 connected gaming communities and there are as many as 20 million registered gamers on the platform. This shows that Enjin is really a serious project to keep an eye on.

Enjin connects games

In many games, players can buy stuff from each other that makes their character better in the game. A well-known example of this is the game RuneScape, where you can, for example, buy a sword to become stronger. These swords are unique to this game and therefore cannot be used in another game such as League of Legends.

But, how nice would it be if you could exchange your sword for runes in League of Legends (this is an element in League of Legends that makes your character better). Or if you're more of a FIFA fan, you could turn in your sword in exchange for Cristiano Ronaldo on FIFA. Enjin's platform aims to enable the union between games. They do this by tokenizing the assets of a game, in this case the sword, the runes and Cristiano Ronaldo.

Turn game items into tokens
In many games, players can buy stuff from each other that makes their character better in the game. A well-known example of this is the game RuneScape, where you can, for example, buy a sword to become stronger. These swords are unique to this game and therefore cannot be used in another game such as League of Legends.

But, how nice would it be if you could exchange your sword for runes in League of Legends (this is an element in League of Legends that makes your character better). Or if you're more of a FIFA fan, you could turn in your sword in exchange for Cristiano Ronaldo on FIFA. Enjin's platform aims to enable the union between games. They do this by tokenizing the assets of a game, in this case the sword, the runes and Cristiano Ronaldo.

What possibilities does the Enjin coin offer?

- **Upgrading existing games**
  In addition to creating your own games, as a game developer you can also choose to upgrade an existing game. Enjin offers Software Development Kits (SDKs) with which you can integrate blockchain technology into already published games.

  This can bring down costs and is a way to combat fraud. In many games there is a lot of "gold farming" going on, where traders make big money trading game money.
  These gold farmers wreak havoc on the game's economy and the creators have no idea of the money flows involved. With blockchain technology all transactions are transparent and everyone can see how the money flows.

- **Creating decentralized games**
  Because Enjin Coin is based on Ethereum's blockchain, you can use smart contracts to make games work decentrally. This means that a game

works completely autonomously and everything is automatically controlled by programming code.

- **Stimulating the player**
  On Enjin's platform you can create your own tokens for your game. Since it is your game, you can also decide what function you want to give the token. An example of this could be that for the soccer game FIFA you create the so-called FIFA tokens. You set up in advance that the winners of a soccer match will win 100 FIFA tokens and that these tokens represent a combined value of 1 Euro. In this way you create an extra incentive for your players and this can benefit gameplay.

- **Rewarding community members**
  You can also use your own token to ensure that you grow your gaming community. For example, you can give members tokens when they have been online for 30 days in a row or when they have introduced new members. These tokens can then also be sold for euros and thus represent real value.

Benefits of Enjin Coin

1. **Blockchain technology brings security and trust to the gaming industry.** Today's games are highly sophisticated and players want their data to be properly secured. Blockchain is the perfect technology for this.

2. **You truly own a gaming asset and can also exchange it for other assets within different games.** You can even choose to create your own new item and insert it into the game.

3. **They offer a Software Development Kit specifically for gaming developers.** This allows existing games to be improved and new games to be created based on blockchain technology.

4. **Enjin offers a solution to fraud within games.** Scammers are often active who use clever tricks to take your game money. Thanks to the security and transparency of blockchain, this is now a lot harder.

5. **Game assets get real value.** Thanks to the Enjin platform you can exchange your assets for real money or assets from other games.

6. **You can create your own assets and introduce them into the game.** You can then earn money with these assets.

7. **Game developers can create their own token and stimulate players and community members.** You can melt the token that belongs to the game into Enjin Coins and sell them for euros.

The Token of Enjin Coin: ENJ

The Enjin coin is based on Ethereum's network and is therefore an ERC20 token. This also allows the coin to be used for smart contracts. Enjin is one of the first projects to adopt Ethereum's Raiden Network. This network is similar to Bitcoin's Lightning Network, but for Ethereum. This network allows the platform to process more transactions.

Distribution of the token
In November 2017, the team raised money through an Initial Coin Offering (ICO). During this coin offering, they were keen to raise $25 million and they managed to reach the 23 million mark. 80% of the total number of coins were sold during this ICO and the remaining 20% was distributed among the team, advisors and the various reward programs.

Suitable wallet for the token
ENJ can be stored on a hardware wallet as well as on the exchange. This is recommended in most cases since you own the private key and are therefore the actual owner of the coins. The best known hardware wallet at this moment is the Ledger Nano S.

Enjin also has its own crypto wallet and it also supports Bitcoin, Ethereum, Litecoin and ERC20, ERC721 and ERC1155 tokens. It is available for both Android and IOS.

Will Enjin Coin get its own blockchain?
Currently, the Enjin Coin is based on Ethereum's blockchain. For now, there are no plans to create their own blockchain. Perhaps they will work on this in the future, but unfortunately due to the lack of the 2021 Roadmap, we do not have a view on this for now.

Competitors
The biggest competitors for Enjin Coin are GameCredits and WAX.
According to Enjin, there is a substantial difference between the two though. Its CMO, Elija Rolovic, says that Enjin Coin is the "Ethereum of Gaming" and its competitors are simple centralized games/marketplaces that happen to carry crypto-currencies. By the sounds of it, there is a healthy rivalry.

Enjin Coin adds the benefits of blockchain to the ever-expanding gaming industry. With a large existing company behind the project and a successful ICO, the financial resources should be good. Whether the team will deliver on its plans remains to be seen. It is unfortunate that they have not yet published a roadmap for 2019. This way we do not know what they are working on. But, a tech giant like Samsung obviously doesn't go into business with just any company, so that's a very positive sign.

Flow Blockchain (FLOW)

NFTs have been around for longer than you might think. In recent months, Non-Fungible Tokens have been wildly popular again, but this hype was also there in 2017-2018. Back then, the blockchain game CryptoKitties was extremely popular.

So popular, in fact, that the Ethereum blockchain on which CryptoKitties sat could no longer handle the number of transactions, with the result that the transaction costs rose dramatically.

The developers of CryptoKitties were dissatisfied with the performance of the Ethereum blockchain and started to develop their own blockchain: Flow Blockchain (FLOW). Flow is a new blockchain built for the next generation of apps, games and the digital assets that power them.

Flow is thus a blockchain aimed at what Ethereum was not for CryptoKitties in 2017-2018. The blockchain is designed to be fast, scalable, decentralized and easy for developers to build on.

Flow thus wants to become the blockchain for developers to build apps, games and digital assets on. The Flow Playground makes it as easy as possible for developers to do this.

There are four pillars that set Flow apart from other blockchains:

- Unique blockchain architecture with 4 roles - scalability without sharding.

- Collector nodes increase network efficiency.

- Execution nodes provide speed and scalability

- Verification nodes guarantee the correctness of the data on the blockchain

- Consensus nodes ensure decentralization

- Easy to use programming language called Cadence

- Customer-friendly interface - Flow accounts make it easy to pay transaction fees and recover lost private keys for users

Flow has since created an impressive community of partners with partners such as NBA, UFC and Ubisoft.

Decentraland (MANA).

The third promising NFT crypto project is Decentraland (LAND & MANA). Decentraland is exactly what you would expect if you read the name carefully: it is a decentralized virtual reality world powered by the Ethereum blockchain.

Within the Decentraland platform, users can create, experience and generate revenue from content and applications. Broadly speaking, it is similar to Sims, Simcity and Second Life, but with a distinct difference: the world is decentralized and is built on the Ethereum blockchain.

Decentraland has two tokens: an ERC-721 Non-Fungible Token, called LAND, and a 'normal' ERC-20 token, called MANA, which is used as the in-game crypto currency. The world of Decentraland, the 'Metaverse', is divided into 90,601 pieces of LAND called parcels. Each parcel is 16m by 16m in size.

The virtual 3D space within Decentraland is called LAND. LAND can be purchased as a player with MANA. The Ethereum blockchain keeps track of who owns which piece of LAND. Important to know is that the world of Decentraland cannot get bigger or smaller.

Owners of LAND therefore own a virtual piece of property in the form of a Non-Fungible Token. On this piece of land within the virtual world of Decentraland, owners can do and make whatever they want: they are the owner of that piece of land.

LAND owners can thus start building on their own piece of the virtual world. By means of the software developer kits of Decentraland, LAND owners can easily build things like static 3D scenes, but also interactive applications and games.

What also often happens is that digital art in the form of an NFT is placed on a piece of LAND. Players can then purchase this digital art with MANA.

The Metaverse, as mentioned above, only consists of about 90000 pieces of LAND. This creates scarcity and causes the price of a piece of LAND to go up, just like it is more expensive to live in New York than in Ohio.

In the Decentraland Marketplace you can view and buy the virtual pieces of land. At this moment the cheapest piece of LAND is for sale for 9440 MANA. Converted to dollars that would amount to around $4000.

In addition to LAND, players can also purchase or earn collectibles, such as an outfit, by participating in special events. These in-game items are also tokenized, which means that there is a token attached. In this case, these are Non-Fungible Tokens.

Finally, what makes Decentraland unique is their DAO. DAO stands for Decentralized Autonomous Orginization. A DAO can actually be seen as a government that operates on the basis of smart contracts. Through the DAO, the user has control over the policies that are put in place to determine how the world behaves.

For example, they decide what types of portable items are allowed and they go over content moderation, LAND policies and auctions. Every participant in the Decentraland network can vote with their Ethereum wallet. The impact power of your vote depends on how much MANA and how much LAND you own.

All in all, Decentraland is an NFT cryptoproject because it is not primarily about collectibles or digital art, but digital real estate in the form of a Non-Fungible Token. The crypto project has been around for a number of years, but to this day it is undergoing a lot of rebuilding.

Worldwide Asset eXchange (WAX)

From digital real estate in the form of NFTs, we are now moving to a marketplace for NFTs. The Worldwide Asset eXchange, known as WAX, calls itself the safest and most convenient way to create, buy, sell and trade virtual items - for anyone, anywhere in the world. WAX has built a platform focused on creating efficient transactions using blockchain technology.

WAX focuses its efforts on making transactions on their network as smooth, efficient and secure as possible.

The game industry is huge. Globally, more than $50 billion worth of in-game items are sold by 500 million players each year. WAX is a marketplace for digital assets and serves over 400 million online players who sell, buy and collect in-game items.

So you can compare it to a Bol.com or an Amazon focused on the Non-Fungible Tokens market. WAX provides smooth and fast transactions using a Delegated Proof Of Stake consensus algorithm. Read more about the Delegated Proof Of Stake consensus algorithm here.

The WAX ecosystem is focused on the game industry and digital collectibles. Through the WAX network, users truly own their digital collectibles or in-game items. So in broad terms, this is similar to Enjin Coin. What makes WAX unique is their NFT creator kit that makes it very easy for developers to tokenize products in the form of a Non-Fungible Token.

In addition, the team at WAX consists of employees with years of experience in the gaming industry. In fact, WAX was founded by OPSkins. OPSkins was the world's largest marketplace for securely buying and selling digital items.

The WAX platform is already in full use. For example, Deadmou5, a house and dubstep producer, has sold his NFTs on the NFT crypto platform.

The Sandbox (SAND)

An NFT crypto project that is competing with Decentraland is The Sandbox (SAND). The Sandbox, like Decentraland, is a virtual world where players can build, own and make money with things on the Ethereum blockchain using SAND, the platform's crypto currency. Sandbox distinguishes itself from Decentraland with a world very similar to Minecraft and Roblox.

Because the game runs on the Ethereum blockchain and all in-game items can be tokenized in the form of NFTs, the game allows users to have real ownership of their creations. In addition, players are rewarded for their participation in The Sandbox world's ERC-20 exchangeable cryptocurrency called SAND.

The game is currently still in development and is expected sometime this year.

In today's game market, the content created by players is still owned by the developers of the game, and not by the players who built the content in the game. If someone builds a gigantic and super interactive world in Minecraft they still do not own that world, that is the developer of the game.

In addition, centralized control over the trade of in-game items made by players limits the real value for their creations. Moreover, it can be difficult to prove ownership of creations: there is no real proof that you were the first to build such a world in Minecraft.

The Sandbox wants to put an end to this by tokenizing all in-game items in the form of Non-Fungible Tokens (NFT). The Sandbox ecosystem consists of 3 elements.

Voxel Editor

The Voxel Editor is an easy-to-use 3D modeling program that allows players to create in-game 3D objects such as puppets, animals, plants, buildings and tools. These 3D objects, once built, become a Non-Fungible Token called ASSETS. These ASSETS can be bought and sold in the Marketplace of The Sandbox.

Marketplace

In The Sandbox Marketplace, users can upload, publish and sell their creations (ASSETS) as NFTs (both ERC-721 and ERC-1155 crypto tokens). They can also view and purchase other players' ASSETS here.

Game Maker mode

The last and also most important part of the Sandbox ecosystem is the game itself. Similar to Decentraland, the virtual space in the world of The Sandbox is divided into ERC-721 Non-Fungible Tokens called LAND. Through Game Maker mode, users can easily "drag" their ASSETS into the world when they have a piece of LAND. This allows players to decorate and customize their own land as they see fit.

By using NFTs, The users from Sandbox will have access to certain benefits such as:

- Real digital property of in-game possessions.

- Security and irremovability of in-game possessions.

- Trade between digital possessions without an intermediary.

- Interoperability between different games: ASSETS, LAND and other game elements can be used in other games.

The crypto currency SAND is the focus of The Sandbox. As with Decentraland, the SAND token can be used for voting through the DAO. In addition, SAND holders can also stake their SAND to generate passive income.

Splyt: Combining e-commerce & NFTs

Splyt is an NFT infrastructure to power decentralized financial & e-commerce markets. Its biggest strength is its focus on e-commerce platforms. The project takes the current NFT hype and turns it into a real use case.

While many projects use NFTs only as collectibles, Splyt gives each NFT a function within a supply chain.

How, you might ask? The core of the project is pretty simple. Each item in an inventory of an online store is marked with its own NFT, or eNFT as Splyt likes to call it. In doing so, the protocol creates a better and more efficient e-commerce system that helps buyers, sellers and marketplaces save time and money by automating key intermediary functions.

By uploading their entire inventory to the Splyt ecosystem, each seller can encourage others to sell their products and automatically pay them a commission to do so.

Anyone can create a Shopify - Powered by Splyt online store and begin selling products available in the Splyt system.

Connecting to Splyt not only has supply chain management benefits, but greatly increases the reach of sellers. And that is ultimately the most important aspect of e-commerce, reaching the customer.

Every item can be easily traced back to its origin and through every step of the supply chain, showing the customer an open and transparent process.

The blockchain technology behind it verifies each step in the process and creates a non-modifiable chain of events.

This allows each customer to know when, where and how the product was created and ultimately brought to their home. This piece of transparency is something that is currently not widely available.

Companies that use the eNTF database system have the following advantages:

- Constant insight into stock both in warehouses and on the road

- Open and transparent attitude towards customers

- Streamlining of affiliate sales by verifying every step in the supply chain

- Dropshipping is more transparent and efficient

The only problem for brands that allow third parties to redistribute their product is the fact that prices are highly inflated and dropshipping stores generally have poor customer service.

The brands will look flawed when the dropshipping store experiences problems, which will be eliminated by using the Splyt protocol.

The actual brand can prove their part of the supply chain, and confirm that the dropshipping store is responsible for the final piece of delivering the product.

The functions of the Splyt protocol

Because Splyt is built on Polkadot, it can enjoy the fast transactions, near-zero transaction fees and instantaneous processing of the Polkadot ecosystem. The underlying technology that Splyt uses is quite complex, and is described in detail in their technical paper. However, we would like to briefly touch on each feature of the Splyt protocol to gain a broader understanding of the company's mission and ambitions;

Global inventory management: With the creation of a unique NFT per item, sellers will know their true inventory at all times. By pushing it all to the blockchain, inventory is constantly verified and made timeless.

Instant Affiliate Payouts: After a successful sale from the global inventory, affiliate sales will receive instant payouts. In the traditional way of affiliate sales, these payouts take long transaction periods due to verification issues. Through blockchain technology, sales can be verified instantly and payments happen instantly.

Universal Reputation System: Everything that happens on a blockchain stays there forever. So, any online store that uses the Splyt protocol will get a certain reputation over time. This increases the order of whether they handle orders correctly, prevent disputes and generally take good care of customers.

Dispute Handling: Any disputes that arise between customer and seller, or between seller and affiliate can be streamlined using the Splyt protocol. Since each step is auditable, confusion is eliminated and disputes can be resolved before they occur.

Real World DeFi Assets: The tokenized inventory can be used as collateral for off-chain decentralized funding. The exact mechanics behind this feature will be shared by the Splyt team at a later stage.

Marketplace Analytics: Everything that happens to a seller's online stores is verified on the blockchain, so on-chain analytics can help sellers maximize sales with smart insights.

The Splyt protocol also offers the Real World DeFi Assets feature, A innovative feature that can be one of the most important components in making Splyt the powerhouse it deserves to be. Liquidity is very important for emerging brands and they often don't have the access to capital they need.

Splyt offers collateralized loans, which can be a very important service for these emerging brands.

These brands can take out loans from the Splyt ecosystem and put up their inventory as collateral, which is stored in centralized storage facilities.

The products are still available to sell online and the borrower repays the amount borrowed. If the borrower defaults on the agreement, Splyt can liquidate the inventory through a Flash sale and close the loan agreement.

The enlarged collateral inventory minimizes the risk involved, the white paper cites an example of a loan for $10,000 on $40,000 of inventory. This varies from case to case and is determined based on data gathered from the market.

The features that we listed above, show the uniqueness and complexity of the Splyt protocol.

While their protocol is diverse, the project chose a clear direction by choosing a select market rather than trying to be a jack-of-all-trades like many other projects.

The $Shop token

At the heart of the protocol is the SHOP token. The token has been brought to life to create incentives for vendors, customers and outsiders alike to continuously maintain and grow the Splyt ecosystem.

Anyone who owns SHOP tokens can earn rewards and have voting rights to decide how the ecosystem continues to evolve.

There are four primary functions of the Shopx token:

- Giving users access to Splyt Core and thereby enabling individuals to buy and sell inventory on the global inventory blockchain.

- Discouraging malicious behavior such as spamming the network, defrauding other members of the ecosystem, or not participating in real world behavior that reflects the agreements on the chain.

- Encouraging participating retailers to bundle inventory redundantly in legacy e-commerce systems, reducing barriers that allow oligopolistic companies to thrive in today's e-commerce regime.

- Compensating individuals, such as arbitrators and listing validators, who help ensure the integrity of the Splyt Core ecosystem in a grassroots environment.

On top of that, SHOP token holders will be able to deploy their tokens in a variety of ways, both short and long, locked and flexible.

Splyt partnerships

The only things that matter to the success of a project these days are the technology, the team and the partnerships. Splyt is nowhere without people actually using their product.

Unlike years ago, when a project like Splyt announced its project without any partnerships, Splyt has now overcome that in a major way. We would like to mention four partnerships in particular.

Maison Du

Maison Du is the partnership that adds the most value to Splyt's proposition. Through Maison Du, an E-Commerce platform for the luxury market, Splyt's first use-case will be to actually deploy its product.

Maison Du is not just another dropshipping store, rather it is a major player in the online retailing world. With 700+ brands, over 1,100 branches and over 1,000 testnet transactions, Maison Du is ready to start using Splyt's product at full scale immediately.

Master Ventures

In early February, Master Ventures officially announced their partnership with Splyt.

The biggest part of the partnership is to hatch Splyt and bring it to the masses.

Over the past few months, it is safe to say that Master Ventures has been quite successful in making this happen. With private sales over 100 times oversubscribed, there is a lot of demand and hype around the project.

In addition, it was Master Ventures that established the connection with the following partner.

Paid Network

What is launching a project without a decent launchpad? Splyt partnered with Paid Network to host their public sale on the Ignition platform.

Lately, Paid has been all over the industry with dozens of partnerships, and a lot of love for their community.

With a community consisting of thousands of members, Splyt is now in the spotlight.

Bridge Mutual

In their most recent partnership with Bridge Mutual, a decentralized discretionary risk coverage platform, Splyt will integrate Bridge Mutual's risk coverage application into their interface.

As stated in their announcement article, This is done by merging their widget onto the Splyt platform to provide a seamless experience for our users, ensuring the ability to purchase coverage for their exchanges without worry.

Splyt began their journey back in 2016 when two founders met and aligned their visions. In 2017, the two began creating the first smart contracts and then years of development followed. Currently, there is a functioning test network that is ready to start moving and accepting users. Their mainnet will appear in the first quarter of 2021.

Looking further down the road, Splyt's current roadmap is not very detailed and large, but it covers the road for the next year. Also, the items listed on the roadmap of Splyt are major milestones that cannot be ignored such as integration with Polkadot, integration with both Shopify and WooCommerce and much more on the horizon.

The future looks bright, but it all comes down to finding the right partners to use the product.

Splyt is a new project with the ambition to reshape E-Commerce by introducing NFTs, using blockchain technology and making the whole process smoother.

The vision is ambitious, but it will all come down to the right execution to see if they can achieve their ambitions. E-Commerce has been a growing trend for years that is open to adapting new technologies, but blockchain technology has yet to merge with this industry.

If Splyt manages to partner with the right companies, gain enough traction, and normalize the use of NFTs, we could potentially see Splyt handle millions of transactions, reaching a large market cap. A key step in this process is their migration to the Polkadot Blockchain.

This will improve transaction speed and reduce the cost of transactions, as Ethereum's Blockchain is currently much slower than Polkadot.

Polkadot (DOT)

Polkadot was started by Dr. Gavin Wood, co-founder of Ethereum and inventor of Solidity, the programming language of smart contracts on the Ethereum blockchain. Wood was frustrated with the rate of progression of Ethereum 2.0 so he started the Web3 Foundation along with Robert Habermeier and Peter Czaban.

Polkadot was subsequently founded by the Web3 Foundation. In late 2017, Web3 Foundation conducted an ICO based on the Polkadot Whitepaper. With the proceeds of this ICO, the Web3 Foundation then went to work. In mid-2019, the Web3 Foundation launched Polkadot's final testnet, called Kusama.

During the Kusama test net period, key elements of Polkadot were tested such as sharding and strike. In May 2020, the first block of Polkadot blockchain was launched; the genesis block.

Polkadot is an open-source sharding-multichain-protocol that enables the cross-chain transfer of data or asset types, so not only tokens, making a wide range of blockchains interoperable with each other.

Quite a technical mouthful, but Polkadot thus distinguishes itself mainly by its unique sharding mechanism, but mainly by allowing different blockchains (cross-chain) to interoperate with each other without problems: interoperability.

This decentralized interoperability between different blockchains helps to shape Polkadot's vision.

How the interoperability of Polkadot works

The main distinguishing feature of Polkadot is cross-chain interoperability. With this interoperability, Polkadot wants to set up a completely decentralized and private network, controlled by its users.

With this network, Polkadot wants to make the creation of new applications and services easier. The network protocol does this by connecting both public and private blockchains, oracles and future technologies.

These independent blockchains are called "parachains." We'll get into this later. This allows these independent blockchains to reliably share information and transactions in the core of the Polkadot blockchain; the relay chain. Again, we will go into this in more detail later.

This makes it possible to build applications with approved data from a private blockchain and use it on a public blockchain.

For example, a school's private, approved academic data can send a certified passing certificate to a smart contract for diploma verification on a public blockchain.

Cross-chain Message Passing: the XCMP protocol

In the future, Polkadot wants to provide more cross-chain interoperability between the different parachains through cross-chain message passing (XCMP). This will allow the independent blockchains, parachains, to connect with each other. XCMP is currently under development and the details are subject to change. Through XCMP, smart contracts from one parachain could trigger a smart contact from another parachain.

The scalability of Polkadot

The number one issue for Bitcoin and cryptocurrency in general is scalability. Many blockchains are currently plagued by slow transaction speeds and high transaction costs.

For example, transaction costs on the Ethereum blockchain are currently incredibly high due to the fact that the Ethereum blockchain is used by the majority of the DeFi sector.

Polkadot was conceived as a solution to the scalability of blockchains like Ethereum, whose transaction throughput is severely limited by the need for each node to validate each transaction.

Polkadot makes use of sharding. Sharding is a technique where not all nodes need to verify every transaction. In fact, transactions are distributed among multiple parts of the network, called shards.

These shards, on the other hand, are known as parachains at Polkadot. Polkadot solves the scalability issue with a blockchain architecture that is one-of-a-kind.

Relay chain and parachains

The Relay Chain is the most significant and central component of Polkadot's architecture. The Relay Chain connects all of the different blockchains or shards on the Polkadot network together. The Relay Chain provides mutual consensus (agreement) between the various blockchains, known as parachains, as well as the previously mentioned cross-chain interoperability.

On the Relay Chain, both of Polkadot's validators stake out DOT tokens and verify for the Relay Chain. The Relay Chain only has a few responsibilities, such as communication with the governance system, parachain auctions, and consensus mechanism involvement. In a moment, we'll go over that in greater depth.

The most critical aspect of the Relay Chain is that it guarantees that transactions from all parachains on the network can be handled in a safe manner at the same time. The network's scalability would improve as a result of this. Other tasks are assigned to the parachains, each of which has its own implementation and features.

Individual blockchains that can provide their own tokens and adapt their features for particular use cases are referred to as parachains. The Relay Chain connects all of the parachains together. Parachains, on the other hand, can be tailored to a specific application.

This means that teams using a parachain have more functionality, performance, and protection than if they used their own general blockchain. Furthermore, by using Substrate, a platform for creating blockchains on Polkadot, teams or businesses can drastically reduce the time it takes to create a blockchain.

Validators attached to the Relay Chain verify the data in the Parachain. It's also worth mentioning that the Relay Chain cannot be linked to an infinite number of parachains.

Polkadot only funds a small number of parachains, estimated to be about 100 at the moment.

Polkadot uses parachain slot auctions, or auctions for short, since the number of slots is small. Auctions on the parachain are just that: auctions.

Parachains-bidders will participate in the auction by indicating their preferred location on the Relay Chain as well as the amount of DOT tokens they are willing to pay.

Parachains bidders can do this out of pocket or use crowdloan functionality to raise DOT from the community.

Polkadot bridges

As indicated earlier, interoperability and cross-chain transfer of data are important features of the Polkadot blockchain. Cross-chain transfer refers to the transfer of data between different independent blockchains.

This cross-chain property is created, among other things, by the so-called bridges. Bridges, or blockchain bridges, are ways in which two independent and technologically different blockchains can communicate with each other.

For example, the Bitcoin blockchain or the Ethereum blockchain can be connected to the Polkadot network via a bridge.

Polkadot's algorithm of consensus
With blockchain currencies, it's important that all data on the blockchain is agreed upon by all network members (nodes). In other words, all network participants must agree that the information on the blockchain is accurate.

The consensus algorithm is used to do this. More information on consensus algorithms can be found here. Polkadot employs a one-of-a-kind consensus algorithm known as Nominated Proof of Stake (NPoS). This is a variant on the Proof of Stake system.

Nominators
The Relay Chain is secured by nominators selecting trustworthy validators and staking DOT. You can become a nominator if you are a DOT token user and holder who wants to win more DOT by striking but don't want to take on the burden of running a node that must be online 24 hours a day, 7 days a week.

Validators
Validators protect the Relay Chain by staking DOT, validating block certificates from collators, and collaborating with other validators to reach consensus. Polkadot's device selects validators a few times per day. In the coming hours, those validators will play a critical role in highly sensitive protocols like block creation.

Collators
Collators maintain a full node of one specific Parachain. That means they retain all the information needed to write new blocks and perform transactions. Under normal circumstances, they will collect and execute transactions to create an unsealed block and provide this, along with a proof of state transition, to the validators responsible for proposing a Parachain block.

Because they are full-fledged nodes, each Collator knows each other as peers. This makes it possible for them to send messages from parachain A to parachain B; interoperability.

Fishermen

Fishermen will be added to the Polkadot network in the future, but they are not currently accessible. The duty of the fishermen is to keep an eye on the Collators. As a result, they track the process of creating new blocks and transactions to ensure that no invalid state changes are included.

The governance of Polkadot

Polkadot (DOT) stands out even more in terms of how its government, or governance, is organized. The governance of a cryptocurrency is concerned with its future: any network enhancements and modifications.

Upgrading a blockchain in other cryptocurrencies is often a complicated and time-consuming method. In reality, a so-called hard fork is frequently the product of an upgrade.

A hard fork can take months to complete and can even cause a crypto community to disintegrate. The hard fork of Bitcoin Cash is an example of this (BCH). A significant portion of the Bitcoin Cash group was originally a part of the Bitcoin community, but left due to a dispute about Bitcoin's block size.

Polkadot takes a different approach by implementing an open and decentralized governance model that empowers users. This is referred to as "user-driven network governance" or "user-driven network management" by Polkadot. Polkadot's governance is made up of all stakeholders who want to be a part of it.

By voting on referendums with the DOT token, these stakeholders will engage in governance. Referendums are basic voting systems based on DOT tokens that have been staked. Each referendum has a distinct proposal. Referendums can be started in a variety of ways:

- Publicly submitted proposals by the Polkadot community.
- Proposals submitted by the Council.
- Proposals submitted as part of the determination of a previous referendum.
- Emergency proposals submitted by the Technical Committee and approved by the Council.

The Polkadot governance system is made up of the members of the Council, the Technical Committee, and all stakeholders who vote with DOT tokens that have been discontinued.

With their discontinued DOT tokens, DOT token holders will vote on referendums and make public referendum proposals.

The Council is made up of members who have been chosen by DOT holders. Referendums and votes for or against emergency measures are proposed by the Council.

Unlike the Council, the Technical Committee is selected by the Council based on a formal Polkadot Protocol specification rather than by voting.

In collaboration with the Council, the Technical Committee will draft emergency referenda that can be voted on and adopted quickly. These emergency numbers are only to be used in the event of a Polkadot network emergency.

The DOT token

Tokenomics is the study of how tokens work inside a crypto's larger ecosystem. That token in Polkadot's case is the DOT token. Polkadot's ecosystem includes the DOT token in a variety of places, including governance and strike.

DOT Governance

As previously mentioned, the first feature of DOT is to grant DOT holders the ability to monitor the platform's governance. The governance system is responsible for deciding the network's fees (trading costs), adding or removing parachains, and special events such as Polkadot network updates and repairs. Polkadot requires someone with a DOT to take part in governance.

DOT Stakes.

DOT is also used in Polkadot's consensus system: Nominated Proof of Stake, in addition to the governance mechanism (NPoS). Strikes exist to keep the Polkadot network running and to enable legitimate transactions to take place over parachains.

Holders of DOTs strike (deploy) their DOTs in exchange for a reward. In the other hand, if malicious network members do not obey the rules, they will be disciplined. Their stake (deployment) has been revoked.

Polkadot is well on their way to completing their plan. The network was still using Proof of Authority at the time of the crypto's launch, but it has now been successfully operating on the NPoS consensus algorithm for some time.

Polkadot, on the other hand, is far from over. The cryptonamically only consists of the Relay Chain, the network's heart, at the time of writing.

On parachain test nets, the functionality of parachain is currently being rolled out for testing and bug fixing. The first parachain auctions, in which the first official parachains will be selected, will take place in the near future.

Many analysts believe that cryptos that secure a parachain spot would see significant price increases.

Polkadot is one of the best performing altcoins in 2020, which is unsurprising. The cryptocurrency is a very ambitious project that, like Ethereum, aspires to be a new type of internet that connects various blockchains.

Conclusion

You should have a good idea of how to conduct your own risk assessment when it comes to investments, selling and trading NFTs by now. Make sure that before you begin and spend money, make sure you have a plan, take the gas fee in account, do your research, and be eager to learn the value of the digital goods you want to buy.

Don't buy into any hype without knowing what you get for your money, or you might just end up buying an overpriced jpeg that you'll never sell.

Or if you're an artist, we provided our top 5 markets, how to get started selling your NFTs, and reasons why they could be the best option for you to start selling your work as an NFT.

Besides that, and we couldn't repeat this enough; the single most important rules of investing in NFT and selling them is to educate yourself on the hype before you begin.

Let us know what you think of the book, and if it has proven to be useful, please leave us a review so that others can benefit as well.

Thank you for reading our book, and good luck with your future investments and NFT trading!

Our books

Check out our other book to learn more about crypto trading, investing, how to make profit and essential tips and strategies for a fail-proof start in the crypto universe.

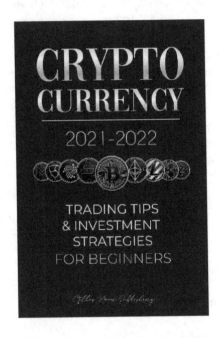

Join the exclusive Stellar Moon Publishing Circle!

You'll get instant access to the mailing list with updates from our experts every week!

Sign up here today:

https://campsite.bio/stellarmoonpublishing